Early County Records
of
Gloucester County
New Jersey

(Slave Documents)

Compiled by:
The New Jersey Historical Records Survey Project

Southern Historical Press, Inc.
Greenville, South Carolina

This volume was reproduced
from a personal copy located in
the Publishers private library

All rights reserved. No part of this publication may be reproduced,
stored in a retrieval system, transmitted in any form, posted
on the web in any form or by any means without the
prior written permission of the publisher.

Please direct all correspondence and book orders to:
SOUTHERN HISTORICAL PRESS, Inc.
1071 Park West Blvd.
Greenville, SC 29611

Published Newark, NJ 1940
ISBN #978-1-63914-614-7
Printed in the United States of America

BIRTH CERTIFICATES

1809.

State of New Jersey
    Gloucester County
        Deptford Township
           Woodbury.

To all whom it may concern:-

           This may certify that "Edward Bellwood" of the aforesaid mentioned Place (Molatto) son of Phebe - (A black woman) the property of Robert Kennedy of the County of Sussex) was born on Friday, the fourteenth day of October in the year of our Lord one thousand eight hundred and eight - 1808. at the House of James Matlack of the County and State aforesaid.
In Testimony whereof I have hereunto set my hand and the eighteenth day of February in the year of our Lord one thousand eight hundred Nine. 1809.

                                    James Matlack

                              [Verso]

Certificate Edward Bellwood
A Male Child - of a Slave

rec'd and filed the 18th day of Feb 7 A D 1809.
Filed 10th February 1809

            C. Ogden Clk.

Birth Certificates

1812.

John, A Male Child of my Negro Slave Betty was born at Camden Gloucester County New Jersey the Twenty ninth day of June eighteen hundred & twelve -

      Edw'd Sharp

Sir:-

  I wish you wou'd record the above and file the same in your office

  I am with respect yours sc

      Edw'd. Sharp

     [Verso]

Mr. Ogden
Clerk of
Gloucester County

Birth Certificates

1819.

State of New Jersey
     Gloucester County Ss
          To the Clerk of the County of Gloucester:-

       I James Matlack of Woodbury in the Township of Deptford, County of Gloucester and State of New Jersey -

       Do by these presents Certify That on thursday the 11th day of March, in the year of our LORD one Thousand eight hundred and nineteen, Was Born of the Body of Sill Johnson (a Black woman) and slave to the subscriber, "a black Female Child, named Dianna Johnson, aged at this time Four weeks and four Days"

       In testimony Whereof I have Set my hand this 12th day of April A. D. eighteen hundred and nineteen - 1819.

                            James Matlack.

                            [Verso]

Certificate of the Birth of a Female black
Child Born Mar. 11th, 1819.
Filed 12th April 1819. Hendry Clk.
Recorded same day - 12 April 1819.

        Hendry Clk.

Birth Certificates

1820.

State of New Jersey
    Gloucester County ^{ss}

To all to whom it may concern:-

I, James Matlack of Woodbury in the County & State aforesaid, do hereby certify that on the Twenty first day of February A D, Eighteen hundred and twenty.

A Female Child named Emaline S. B. Johnson, aged at this time Seven weeks was born of the body of Phebe Johnson a Courlered Woman a Slave the property of the said Matlack - Which certificate is produced to the Clerk of the said County to be recorded this Tenth day of April A D Eighteen hundred and twenty -

                Per
                James Matlack
                April 10th 1820.

[Verso]

Certificate of the Birth of Emaline S. B. Johnson
daughter of Phebe Johnson a slave

Recorded 10 April 1820 in the Book A
of Manumissions Page 6

        Hendry, Clk.

Birth Certificates

5.

1820

State of New Jersey

Gloucester County ss

I Samuel Kille of the Township of Woolwich in the County and State aforesaid do by these presents Certify that on the twenty first day of November in the Year of our Lord, one thousand eight hundred and Nineteen, Was born of the body of Nancy, a Black Woman and Slave to the Subscriber "A Male child named Frank" aged at this time Ten Months and twenty five Days.

In Testimony Whereof I have hereunto Set my hand this Sixteenth day of October A D Eighteen hundred and Twenty

        Samuel Kille

        [Verso]

Certificate Sam Kille
Recorded 16 October 1820 in Book A
Page 10, of Manumissions
    Hendry, Clk.

Birth Certificates

1820.

Gloucester County ss

I William Tod of the township of Waterford County of Gloucester, New Jersey do by these presents Certify that on the third day of August A D 1811 Was born of the Body of Biddy a Black Woman and Slave to the Subscriber a "Female S~~lave~~ "Child" named Mary Ann aged at this time above Nine Years and Four Months

In Witness Whereof I have hereunto Set my hand this thirteenth day of December A D 1820

<u>Willm Tod</u>

Gloucester County ss

I William Tod of the Township of Waterford County of Gloucester New Jersey do by these presents Certify that on the /.../ day of August A D 1818 Was Born of the Body of Biddy, a Black Woman and slave to the subscriber a Male Child Named Paul aged at this time about ~~three~~ Two Years and four Months

In Witness whereof I have hereunto set my hand this thirteenth day of December A D 1820

<u>Willm Tod</u>

/Vers<u>o</u>/

Certificate of the birth of two Slaves to Wm. Tod.

Recd Decem 13 1820 and recorded in the Clerks Office at Woodbury Lib A of Manumissions folio 14

J. J. Foster, Clk.

Birth Certificates

1822.

State of New Jersey

    Gloucester County ss

I William Tod of the township of Waterford, in the County and State aforesaid, do hereby Certify that on the Seventeenth day of March A D eighteen hundred and Twenty Two, a Male Child aged at this time about one week Named Toby Was born of the body of Biddy a Coloured Woman and Slave of the Subscriber's -

Which Certificate is produced to the Clerk of the said County, to be recorded this twenty third day of March A D 1822.

                    Willm Tod

                      [Verso]

Certificate of Male child
named "Toby" Slave of Wm Tod

filed March 22d 1822
    J J Foster Clk

Recorded in Book A of Manumissions
folio 17.

        J. J. Foster, Clk.

Birth Certificates

8.

1825

Vilet a black Girl belonging to John Ingersull was born April 15th 1825

please call on Mr. Smalwood for my deed

John Ingersull

Samuel B. Westcott

/Verso/

Recorded in the Clerk Office of Gloucester County in Liber A of Manumissions fol 25
Sep 2 1833

<u>Smallwood Clk</u>

filed Sep. 2, 1833

<u>Smallwood Clk</u>

```
  17
   2
  --
  34
1770
   8
  ----
1812
```

CERTIFICATES OF MANUMISSIONS

and

AFFIDAVITS OF OWNERS

1788.

Gloucester County ss We do hereby Certify that on this Tenth Day of May Anno Domini One Thousand seven Hundred and Eighty Eight Joseph Hugg of the Town and County of Gloucester brought before us, [...] of the Overseers of the poor of the said Town, [...] two of the Justices of the Peace of the said County his Slave named Berten, Who on View and examination appears to us to be sound in Mind, and not under any bodily incapacity of obtaining a Support, and also is not under twenty one years of Age, nor above thirty five: In Witness wh[...] we have hereunto set our hands the Tenth day of May One Thousand seven Hundred and Eighty Eight 1788.

       John Glover)
       John Heritage) Overseers
       John Sparks)
       John Wilkins) Justices

[Verso]

Recorded in the Clerks
Office Gloucester County 30th May 1788.

  E. Clark Clk

Certificates of Manumissions - Affidavit

1791.

I do hereby Certify that on the twenty-second day of October in the Year of our Lord One thousand seven hundred and eighty nine, my Slave named Jane Shores was brought before Garret Groff and Jacob Lippincott two of the Overseers of the Poor of the Township of Greenwich in the County of Gloucester, and was Manumitted According to Law in the presence of John Wilkins and Jeffery Clark Esquires.

Witness my hand & Seal this 11th day of October 1791.

                    Susannah Taylor (Seal)

[Verso]

                Manumission
Recorded in the Clerks Office of Gloucester County in Lib A folio of Manumission of Slaves.

            E. Clark Clk

Certificates of Manumissions

1789.

New Jersey   )   We do hereby certify that on this Twenty second
Gloucester   )   day of October in the year of our Lord one Thou-
County ss   )   sand seven Hundred & Eighty nine Susannah Taylor
                 of the Township of Greenwich in the sd. County of
Gloucester, brought before us, two of the overseers of the poor of
sd. Township and two of the Justices of the peace of sd. County
her Slave named Jane Shores who on view & examination appears to
us to be sound in Mind, and not under any Bodily Incapacity of
obtaining a support, and also is not under the age of Twenty one
years, nor above Thirty five; IN WITNESS whereof we have hereunto
set our hands & Seals the day above written.

                              Overseers

                              Garret Groff   (Seal)
                              Jacob Lippincott (Seal)

Justices:-

John Wilkins   (Seal)
Jeffery Clark (Seal)

[Verso]

             Manumission of Wm. Taylers Slave
Recorded in the Clerks Office of Gloucester County in
Lib A of Manumission of Slaves.

                         E. Clark, Clk.

1/4 dol. each

Certificates of Manumissions

1789

Gloucester County ss

We do hereby Certify that on this seventh day of December in the year of our Lord one Thousand seven Hundred and Eighty nine Hannah Wilkins late Hannah Matlack of the Township of Deptford in the sd County of Gloucester brought before us, two of the Overseers of the poor of sd. Township and two of the Justices of the peace of sd. County, her Slave named Rodger who on View and Examination appears to us to be sound of in Mind and not under any Bodily Incapacity of Obtaining a Support and also is not under twenty one years of Age nor above Thirty five, IN WITNESS whereof we have hereunto set our hands the day above written

Justices
Jos, Blackwood
Jeffery Clark

Jonathan Brown
Peter Crim

/Verso/

      Certificate for Matlachs Negro Rodger
Recd. January 16th 1816 and recorded in the Clerks office in Woodbury, in Lib W folio 456 of Deeds.

Hendry Clk.

Certificates of Manumissions

1791.

Gloucester County ss)

We do hereby certify, that on this Eighteenth day of April in the Year of our Lord One thousand seven hundred and Ninety one, Hugh Greighton of the Township of Newton, in the said County of Gloucester, brought before us, two of the Overseers of the Poor of said Township, and two of the Justices of the Peace of said County, his Mulatto Slave, named Flora, who on view and examination appears to us to be sound in mind, and not under any bodily Incapacity of obtaining a support, and also is not under twenty one Years of Age, nor above thirty five: IN WITNESS whereof wee have hereunto set our Hands the day and Year above written.

Jo: Hugg   ) Justices of
Saml; Kenard) the Peace.

Thomas Redman) Overseers
Thomas Githens) of the Poor.

/Verso/

Certificate of the Freedom of Flora Recorded in the Clerks Office of Gloucester County in Lib A of Manumission of Slaves.

E. Clark, Clk.

Certificates of Manumissions - Affidavit

1791.

I do hereby Certify that on the Seventh Day of October in the year of our Lord one thousand Seven Hundred & Ninty one my Slave Jeff Shores was Brought Before Jacob Gooden & John Early two of the overseers of the Poor of the Township of Greenwich in the County of Gloucester and Was manumated according to Law in the Presents of John Sparks & Thos. Carpenter Esquire, Witness my hand & Seal this Seventh Day of october 1791.

       Jeffery Clark.

       [Verso]

Manumission

Recorded in the Clerks Office of Gloucester County in Lib A of manumission of Slaves

   E. Clark Clk

Certificates of Manumissions

1791.

Gloucester County) We do hereby Certify that on this eleventh
New Jersey SS s   ) day of October in the year of Our Lord One
) thousand seven hundred & Ninety One Jeffery
Clark Esquire of the Township of Greenwich
in the said County of Gloucester brought before us, two of the
overseers of the poor of said Township, and two of the Justices of
the Peace of said County. his Slave named Jeffery Shores who on
View and examination Appears to us to be sound in mind and not
under any bodily incapacity of obtaining a support, and also is
not under twenty one years of Age, nor above thirty five: IN
WITNESS whereof we have hereunto ser Our hands the 11th day of
October 1791

Taken before us the day) Justices   Jacob Goodin (Seal)   ) Overseers
and year above Writen   ) of the   )
      John Sparks (Seal)) Peace   John Earley (Seal)   ) of the
      Thos:Carpenter(Seal)   ) Poor

[Verso]

Manumission
Recorded in the Clerks office of Gloucester
County in Lib A folio of Manumission of Slaves.

E Clark Clk

Certificates of Manumissions

1793

Gloucester County ss

We do hereby Certify that on this Sixteenth day of July in the year of our Lord One thousand seven hundred & Ninety three, Joseph Hugg of the Town of Gloucester, in the County of Gloucester aforesaid Esquire brought before us two of the Overseers of the Poor of said Town, and two of the Justices of the Peace of said County, his Slave named Tabby Still.

Who on view and examination appears to us to be Sound in Mind, and not under any bodily incapacity of obtaining a support, and also is not under twenty one years of Age, nor above thirty five. In Witness whereof we have hereunto set our Hands the Day and Year above written.

Jno Griffyth	) Justices of	John Heritage	) Overseers
Samul Kenard	) the Peace	Peter Thompson	) of the Poor.

[Verso]

Certificate of the Freedom of Joseph Hugg's Negroe Man Tabbey.

Recorded in the Clerks Office of Gloucester County this 19th August 1793

E. Clark Clk

Certificates of Manumissions

17.

1794.

Gloucester County ss   State of New Jersey.

We Doe hereby Certify that on this Eighteenth Day of April in
the year of our Lord one Thousand and Seven hundred and ninty
four Denil Bates of the Township of Gloces in the county aforsd
Brought Before us Two of the overseers of the poor of the sd
Township of Glouester and Two of the Justices of the peace of
Said County - his Slave named Susanath who on View and Exami-
nation appears to us to be Sound in mind and not under any
Bodily Incapacity of obtaining a support and allso is not under
Twenty one years of age nor above Thirty five in Wittness Whereof
we have hereunto Set our hands and Seals, the Day and year above
Written.

          Nathan Lippincott (Seal)

          Daniel Bates (Seal)

We the underwritten two of the
Justices of said County Do ap-
prove of the above.

    John Sparks
    Jo. Hugg.

[Verso]

     Manumission of Dane Bates & Susanath

Recorded in Clerks Office of Gloucester County in Page - 24th
April 1794

    E. Clark Clk

Certificates of Manumissions

1794.

Month /. . . . ./
ten /. . . . . . ._. . . . ./ ./
faithfully /. . . ./. . . . ./ ./
honestly, order /. /. . . . ./ ./
Mistress, and /. ._. . . . ./ ./
his Self, his Ex /. ._. . . . ./ ./
the said John Spar /. ._. . . . ./ ./
Folwell & Rachel his /. ._. . . . ./ ./
of all manner of House /. ._. . . . ./ ./
knitting, etc. shall and /. ._. . . . ./ ./
tice nine months Schooling /. ._. . . . ./ ./
unto the said Apprentice con /. . . . ._. . . . . . ./ ./
and all other things necessary and /. ._. . . . . . ./ aforesaid
and at the end of the said Term shall /. . . . ./ Apprentice two
good suits of Aprel of all sorts both linen & Woolen, one whereof to
be new, the other for working Apparel. AND the said Samuel Folwell
for his Self, his Executors and Administrators, hereby Covenants to
and with the said John Sparks his Heirs, Executors & Administratore, that
he the said Samuel Folwell his Executors of Administrators shall and will
Manumit and set the adoresaid Apprentice named Rachel Absolutely Free
at the end of the aforesaid Term, giving up unto her all his and their
right and claim whatsoever, as to her person and-all-the-issue-that-may
of-her-Body-be-begotten, and any Estate she or-they may thereafter acquire.
AND the said John Sparks the better to impower the said Samuel Folwell
his Executors or Administrators to Manumit the said Negro Girl. doth hereby forever release unto the said Samuel Folwell his Executors and Administrators all his right and claim whatsoever in and to the person of the
said Negro Rachel Freeman; Hereby declaring, she (together-with-all-and
every-the-issue-of-her-Body-that-may-be-begotten) shall be Manumitted and
set absolutely FREE from BONDAGE, without any interuption, at the end of
the adoresaid Term, from all and every person whomsoever claiming.
IN WITNESS whereof the parties to these Presents have hereunto interchang-
eably set their Hands and Seals, DATED the fourteenth Day of the Eight
Month (August) Ano Domini one thousand seven hundred and ninety four.

SEALED & DELIVERED in the Presence of   (Seal)

Memorandum, The Words "and all the issue that may of her Body be begotten,"
and the Words "or they", and the Words "together with all and every the
issue of her Body that may be" "begotten,"- were all erased with a Pen,
between the 26th & 34th lines, before the Executing thereof.

/Verso/

A coppey of asertificat of Abratham Deval & Sarath
Clark now Sarath Deval

| | torn | 5,35 20 2 5 1/4 | 76 8 10 3/47 | 11111111-1111111- | 277.10 33.15 — 311.5 11 | 740 225 37.10 — 262.10 15 — 277.10 |

Certificates of Manumissions

1798.

Kent County State Maryland.

To all whom these presence shall come Greetings:-

Know ye that I Ann Cobourn of the County and State aforesaid, for whom good Causes and Consideration me thereto moving do hereby declare free, Manumitt, and Enfranchise a negro man called Joe and hereby Acknowledge /.../ Said Joe, is charged from all claim of Survice and right of property, Whatever from me my heirs Executors administrators /.../ As Witness my hand and seal this Ninth day of March in the year of our Lord one thousand Seven hundred and Ninty Eight

            Ann Coburn (Seal)

Witness William Harris
and Joseph William

In Test /.../ whereof /.../ have this /.../ in the year of Lord Eighteen hundred and nine and /.../ affixed the seal of my office.

      Attest Ben Chambers

Certificates of Manumissions

1799.

Gloucester County to Wit) We do hereby Certify that on this
24 Day of august in the year of our
Lord one thousand Seven Hundred and
Ninty Nine William Eldradge of the Township of Greenwich in the
said County of Gloucester Brought before us Two of the overseers
of the Poor of the said Township and Two of the Justices of the
Peace of the County his Slave Sarah Green Who on View and Examination
appears to us to be Sound in Mind and not under any bodily Incapacity
of Obtaining a Support and also in not under the age of Twenty one
years nor above the age of Forty years in Witness Were of We have
hereunto Set our hands, the Day & year above Written.

    James C. Wood   ) Overseers of the Poor
    Thomas Reeves   ) of the Township

    Jeffery Clark   ) Justices of the Peace of
    I Pine   ) the said County.

[Verso]

Sarah Green
Surtificate for
Wm. Eldredge
    Negro.

Recorded.

Certificates of Manumissions

1800.

To Whom It May Concern

        Know Ye that my Negro Woman Named Tenvi Freeman, Aged twenty six Years and Upwards, Is hereby Manumitted, Discharged and set free. WITNESS my Hand and seal the Ninth day of January in the Year of Our Lord Eighteen Hundred 1800.

Witness Present   John Sparks   (Seal)
    Elisha Clark

Gloucester County : ss We do hereby certify that on this Ninth Day of December in the Year of Our Lord Eighteen Hundred John Sparks Esq. of the said County of Gloucester brought Before us the Subscribers two of the Overseers of the poor of the Township of Deptford and two Justices of the peace of said County his Negro Woman a Slave Named Tenvi Freeman Who on View and Examination Appeared to us to be sound in Mind and not Under any Bodily Incapacity of Obtaining a Support, and also is not Under Twenty one Years of Age nor above thirty five, In Witness Whereof We have hereunto set our Hands the Day and Year above Written.

Ja. Hopkins   Justice   Thomas Reeves
Jno. Blackwood   Justice   Levi Hooper
                                               Overseer of the poor

[Verso]

Tenvi Freeman discharge

Recorded in the Clerks Office of
the County of Gloucester.

     E Clark Clk

Certificates of Manumissions

1803.

To Whom it may Concern - Know ye that I James B. Caldwell by the Authority given me by Solomon Combs in a Certain Indenture Given to John Lawrence on a Negro Woman named Rose bearing date 30th March 1798 In which Indenture sd Combs hath particularly specified that the sd Rose should be manumitted and set free - do hereby Manumit discharge and set free the aforesaid Negro Woman Rose aged about thirty three years being the property of said Solomon Combs - Witness my hand seal the third day of December Eighteen hundred and three -

            James B. Caldwell.

Gloucester County to wit, We do hereby Certify that on the third day of December Eighteen hundred and three James B. Caldwell agreeable to an Indenture given to John Lawrence bearing date March 30th 1798 by Solomon Combs on a Certain Negro Woman named Rose in which Indenture sd Combs hath particularly specified that the sd Negro Woman Rose should be manumited and set free Brought before us the subscribers the only acting overseer of the poor of the township of Debtford and two of the Justices of the Peace of the sd County the aforesaid Negro Woman named Rose the Property of sd Solomon Combs.
Which sd Rose on View and examination appears to us to be sound in Mind and not under any Bodily incapacity of obtaining a support and also is not under the age of twenty one years nor above the age of forty years - In Witness Whereof we have hereunto set our hands the day & year above written.

Acting overseer of the poor of the township of Debtford	As Justices of the peace of the County of Gloucester
Biddle Reeves	Jonathan Harker, J. P.
	Jeremiah Wood.

[Verso]

Rose's Manumission

Recorded 6th decem 1803 in the Clerks Office of Gloucester County in Book A.

   E Clark Clk

Certificates of Manumissions

1803

Gloucester County) To wit.

We do hereby Certify that on this 14th day of April in the year of our Lord one Thousand Eight hundred and three Isaac Mickel Esq. of the Township of Newton in the County afsd brought before us two of the Overseers of the Poor of the said Township and two of the Justices of the peace of said County, his Slave named Sharper who on view and examination appears to be sound in Mind, and not under any Bodily incapacity of obtaining a support and is not under the Age of twenty one years nor above the age of Forty years. In Witness Whereof we have hereunto set our hands the day and year first above written.

    John Rowand) Overseeing the Poor of the Township
    Joseph Evens) of Newton.

    Joseph Champion) Justices of the peace in & for
    J. Clement   ) the said County of Gloucester.

[Verso]

    Certificate of Manumission of
    Isaac Mickel Esq. Slave Sharper.

Recorded in the Clerks Office of Gloucester County 17 May 1803.

    E Clark Clk

Paid

Certificates of Manumissions

1804.

Gloucester County to wit:- We do hereby Certify that on this Fifth day of September in the year of our Lord one thousand Eight hundred & four Samuel W. Harrison of the Town of Gloucester in the said County of Gloucester brought before us two of the overseers of the poor of the said Township, and two of the justices of the peace of the said County, his Slave named Ceasar Smith who, on view and examination appears to us to be sound in mind, and not under any bodily incapacity of obtaining a support and also is not under the age of twenty one years, nor above the age of forty years. In Witness whereof we have hereunto set our hands, the day and year above written.

       John Heritage   )   Overseers of the poor of the
       Saml Bricke   )   Town of Gloucester.

Jonathon Harker   )   Justices of the peace for
James Matlack   )   the said County of Gloucester

/Verso/

                  Manumission of
                  Cesar Smith.

Recorded in the Clerks Office of Gloucester
County May 8, 1805

       Clark Clk

Certificates of Manumissions

1504*

Gloucester County to wit, We do hereby Certify that on this Eighth day of September in the year of our Lord one thousand Fifth hundred & four Samuel W. Harrison of the Town of Gloucester in the County of Gloucester brought before us (two of the Overseers of the poor of the said Town and two of the Justices of the peace of the said County.) his slave named Thomas Smithers who on view and examination appears to us to be sound in mind and not under any bodily incapacity of obtaining a support and also is not under the Age of twenty one years nor above the Age of forty years In Witness whereof we have hereunto set Our hands the day and year above written.

   John Heritage) Overseers of the poor of the

   Sam Brick   ) Town of Gloucester.

Jonathan Harker)
) Justices of the peace for the
James Matlack) County of Gloucester.

        /Verso/

      Manumission of
      Thomas Smithers

Recorded in the Clerks Office of Gloucester
County May 8th 1805

     Clark Clk

---

* Dates in manumission are the result of an error by clerk. Actual dates should be 1804.

Certificates of Manumissions

1704*

Gloucester County to wit - We do hereby Certify that on this Fifth day of September in the year of our Lord one thousand seven hundred a four George W Hugg of the Town of Gloucester in the said County of Gloucester brought before us two of the Overseers of the poor of the said Town and two of the Justices of the peace of the said County his Slave named Cupied Still who in view and examination appears to be sound in mind and not under any bodily incapacity of obtaining a support and also is not under the Age of twenty one years, nor above the age of forty years. In Witness whereof we have hereunto subscribed our hand the Day and Year above written.

John Heritage) Overseers of the poor of the
Sam Brick   ) Town of Gloucester

Jonathan Harker) Justices of the peace of the
James Matlack   ) County of Gloucester

[Verso]

Manumission of Cupied Still

Recorded in Clerk's Office of Gloucester County
    May 8, 1805
            Clark Clk

---

* Dates in manumission are the result of an error by clerk. Actual dates should be 1804.

Certificates of Manumissions - Affidavit

1805

We John Stokes and Jacob Stokes Executors of the Last Will and Testament of Jacob Stokes, late of the Township of Newton, in the County of Gloucester in the State of New Jersey, Yeoman, deceased, and Heirs at Law of the said Jacob Stokes, Do hereby set free from Bondage, Our two Negroes, late part of the said Estate, to wit Fanny Smothers Aged about twenty five Years, and Pero Fisher aged about twenty two years, and do for ourselves, our Executors, and Administrators, release unto the said Fanny, and Pero, all our right, and all claim whatsoever as to their persons, or to any Estate they or either of them may Acquire hereby declaring the said Fanny & Pero, absolutely free without any interruption from us, or any person claiming under us. In Witness whereof we have hereunto set our hands and Seals, the fourteenth day of May in the Year of our Lord One thousand eight hundred and five, 1805

Sealed and Delivered)
in the presence of us)
   Thomas Redman   )
   Joseph Green   )

John Stokes   (Seal)

Jacob Stokes (Seal)

[Verso]

Be it Remembered that on the third day of October 1807. personally came before me James Hopkins Esq. one of the Judges of the inferior Court of Common Pleas in and for the County of Gloucester; John Stokes one of the Grantors of the within written Manumission and Acknowledged that he Signed Sealed and Delivered the same for the uses and purposes therein contained; and also personally came before me Thomas Redman one of the within subscribers Witness, who being one of the people called Quakers, upon his Solemn Affirmation saith that he saw Jacob Stokes the other Grantor of the within Manumission Sign, Seal and deliver the same for the Uses & purposes, therein contained, and that Joseph Evens the other within subscribing witness was also present and subscribed his Name at the same time, Witness his Hand

Taken and Affirmed the Day and)
Year above written.) Thomas Redman
Before me)

   Jos. Hopkins

               Manumission
          John Stokes & Jacob Stokes
                   of
         Fanny Smothers & Pero Fisher

Certificates of Manumissions

1805

Gloucester County ss)

                          We do hereby Certify, that on this fourteenth day of May, in the Year of our Lord one thousand eight hundred and five, John Stokes & Jacob Stokes of this Township of Newton, in the County aforesaid, Executors of the Last Will and Testament of Jacob Stokes late of Newton aforesaid, deceased, and Heirs at law of the said Jacob Stokes, brought before us, two of the Overseers of the Poor of said Township, and two of the Justices of the Peace of said County, their two Negro Slaves late the property of said Estate - to wit - Fanny Smothers & Pero Fisher, who on view and examination, appear to us, to be sound in mind and not under any bodily incapacity of obtaining a Support, and also are not under twenty one Years of Age, nor above thirty five. In Witness whereof we have hereunto set our hands the day and year above written.

Joseph Evens	)	Overseer of the Poor of the
Isaac Webster	)	said Township of Newton.
Joseph Champion	)	Justices of the Peace in & for
John Clement	)	the said County of Gloucester.

[Verso]

Certificate of the Freedom
of Fanny Smothers & Pero Fisher.

filed 8th October 1807

        C Ogden Clk

Recorded in the Clerks Office of Gloucester County in Lib A of manumission October 8th 1807

        C Ogden Clk

Certificates of Manumissions

1806

State of New Jersey, Gloucester County.

We certify that on this Twenty third day of June in the year of our Lord, One thousand eight hundred and six, James Stratton of the Township of Woolwich in the said County of Gloucester, brought before us, two of the Overseers of the Poor of the said Township, and two of the Justices of the peace of the said County, his Slave named, Ishmael, who, on view and examination, appears to us to be, sound in mind, and not under any bodily incapacity, of obtaining a support, and also is not under the age of twenty one years, nor above the age of forty years. In Witness whereof we have hereunto set our hands, the day and year above written.

                              Overseers of the Poor of the
                              Township of Woolwich

                              Samuel Paul
                              Samuel Lippincott.

Justices of the Peace in and for the
County of Gloucester
    Nicholas Justice   )
    Rich'd Fittermary) J. Peace.

[Verso]

                      Certificate for
                      Mulatto Ishmael

Recorded in the Clerks Office of Gloucester County in Lib A of Manumission of Slaves November 22d, 1806.

                    C. Ogden Clk

Certificates of Manumissions - Affidavits

1807.

Gloucester ss   State of New Jersey

To all whom these Presents shall come Greeting,
It is hereby made known that on this third day of October in the year of our Lord One thousand eight hundred and Seven I John Stokes of the Township of Newton in said County of Gloucester and I Abigail Stokes Widow of Jacob Stokes late of said Township Deceased, have liberated manumited and set free our Negro Slave called Mina of the Age of Twenty One Years of thereabouts, And we hereby liberate Manumit and Set free our said Negro Slave and discharge her from all service or demand of Service to be hereafter made either by us or any Person Claiming by from or under us -

In Testimony whereof we have hereunto set our hands and seals the day and year aforesaid

Sealed and Delivered
in the Presence of us

                                           John Stoked   (Seal)

                                           Abbey Stokes   (Seal)

Isaac Webster

John Clement

[Verso]

Gloucester County ss) On the third day of October in the year of our Lord one thousand eight hundred and Seven came before me the Subscriber one of the Judges of the Court of common please in and for said County John Stokes and Abigail Stokes the makers and granters of the written Manumission and Acknowledged they executed the same for the uses and purposes therein mentioned.

Taken and Acknowledged)   John Clement
before me   )

Manumission John Stokes &
Abigail Stokes of Mina Black
Woman

                                    67
                                    20
                                 1340
                                     6
                                    78
                                    84

Certificates of Manumissions

1807.

Gloucester County to wit: We do hereby certify that on the Third day of October in the year of our Lord one thousand eight hundred and Seven - John Stokes of the township of Newton in the County of Gloucester and Abigail Stokes widdow of Jacob Stokes of the township aforesaid decd, brought before us two of the Overseers of the poor of the said Township and two of the Justices of the peace of the said County their Slave named Mina - - - who on view and examination appears to us to be sound in mind and not under any bodily incapacity of obtaining a Support and also is not under the age of twenty one years nor above the age of forty years. In witness whereof we have hereunto Set our hand the day and year above written.

  Robert Rowand) Overseers of the poor of the
  Isaac Webster) Said Township Newton.

Jas. Hopkins) Justices of the peace in and for the
John Clement) said County of Gloucester.

/Verso/

  Certificate of the
  Freedom of Mina
  a black Woman.

Recorded in the Clerks Office of
Gloucester County in Lib A of Manumissions
October 8th 1807

  C Ogden Clk

Certificates of Manumissions - Affidavit

1807.

State of New Jersey

Gloucester County ss

    (SEAL)   To all to whom these presents shall come, greeting.

It is hereby made known, that on this eighteenth day of November in the year of our Lord One thousand eight hundred and seven. 1807 I Mary Wood of the Township of Deptford in the said County of Gloucester. have liberated, manumited and set free my negro Slave called George Huggins Mitchfield of the age of twenty one years and I do hereby liberate, manumit and set free, my said negro Slave, and discharge him from all service or demand of service to be hereafter made, either by me or any persons claiming by, from or under me.

In Testimony whereof I have hereunto set my Hand and seal the day and year aforesaid.

Sealed and delivered in the
presence of us

Amos Cooper)
James Matlack) Mary Wood.

Be it remembered that on the 18th day of November in the year of our Lord one thousand eight hundred and Seven before me James Matlack one of the Judges of the Inferior Court of Common Pleas in and for the County of Gloucester Personally appeared Mary Wood, the maker and grantor of the above Manumission, and acknowledged that she signed, sealed and delivered the said Manumission as her voluntary act for the uses and purposes therein mentioned.

                                      Taken and acknowledged Before
                                                     James Matlack

[Verso]

                Manumission of
                from Mary Wood
                November 18th, 1807

Recorded in the Clerks Office of Gloucester County in Book A of manumissions

        C Ogden Clk

Certificates of Manumissions

33.

1807.

State of New Jersey

Gloucester, to wit:

We do hereby certify, that on this eighteenth day of November in the year of our Lord one thousand eight hundred and Seven 1807.

Mary Wood of the township of Deptford in the County of Gloucester, brought before us two of the Overseers of the poor of the said Township, and two of the Justices of the peace of the said County, her Slave named George Huggins Mitchfield who on view and examination, appears to us to be sound in mind, and not under any bodily incapacity of obtaining a support, and also is not under the age of twenty one years, nor above the age of forty years.

In witness whereof we have hereunto set our Hands the day and year above written.

        Overseers of the Poor of the
        Township of Deptford

          Amos Cooper
          Job. Brown

Charles Ogden)
James Matlack) Justices of the peace in and for the said County
       of Gloucester.

         /Verso/

        Certificate of the
        Capacity of
        November 18th, 1807

Recorded in the Clerks Office of Gloucester County
in Lib.A. of Manumissions

       C Ogden Clk

Certificates of Manumissions - Affidavit

1809

Gloucester County ss

To all to whom these presents shall come, it, is hereby made known, that on this Eighteenth day of June in the year of our Lord one thousand Eight hundred and nine, I James Stratton of the Township of Woolwich in the said County of Gloucester, have liberated, manumitted and set free, my Negro Slave, called Marinda Duffield, of the age of Twenty five years or thereabouts: and I do hereby liberate manumit and set free, my said Negro Slave, and discharge her from all service, or demand of service to be hereafter made either by me or any person claiming by from or under me.

In testimony whereof I have hereunto set my hand and seal the day and year aforesaid.

Sealed and Delivered   )
in the presence of   )
) James Stratton. (Seal)
James B. Caldwell   )
William Harrison   )

[Verso]

Gloucester County ss   Be it remembered that on the twentieth day of June in the year of our Lord One thousand Eight hundred and nine, before me the Subscriber one of the Judges of the Court of Common Pleas in and for said County personally appeared James Stratton, the within named grantor, and acknowledged that he did sign seal and deliver the within instrument of manumision as his act and deed, to and for the uses and purposes therein mentioned.

Taken and acknowledged
the day and year aforesaid.

        James B. Caldwell

Certificates of Manumissions

1809.

State of New Jersey

Gloucester County ss

We do hereby certify, that on this Seventeenth day of June in the year of our Lord One thousand, Eight hundred and nine. James Stratton of the Township of Woolwich in the said County of Gloucester, brought before us two of the Overseers of the Poor of the said Township of Woolwich, and two of the Justices of the Peace of the said County of Gloucester, his female Slave named Marinda Duffield, who on view and examination, appears to us to be sound in mind and not under any bodily incapacity of obtaining a support, and also is not under the age of Twenty one years, nor above the age of forty years. In witness whereof we have hereunto set our hands the day and year above written.

            John Lippincott)
            Vanderver Homan) Overseers

            James B. Caldwell
            William Harrison

[Verso]

      Manumission
      Merinda Duffield

Recorded in the Clerks Office of Gloucester County in Lib A of manumission, June 22, 1809

     C Ogden Clk.

Certificates of Manumissions

1811

Gloucester County to wit. We do hereby Certify that on this sixth Day of June one thousand Eight hundred and Eleven John Stokes - and Abigail Stokes - of the township of Newton and County of Gloucester Brought before us two of the Overseers of the Poor of said township, and two of the Justices of the peace of said county their Slave, Name Nences Fisher, who on view and examination appears to us to be sound in mind and not under any Bodily Incapacity of Obtaining a support, and also is not under the age of twenty one years; nor above the age of forty years.

In witness whereof we have hereunto set our hands the Day and Year above written.

Isaac Webster   ) Overseers of
Joseph Middleton) the Poor

Benjamin Burrough)
Joseph Sloan   ) Justices of the
                   Peace

[Verso]

Certificate of the Freedom
of Nenus Fisher
Recorded in the Clerks Office of Gloucester
County Lib A of manumission   June 10, 1812

Recorded   C. Ogden Clk

Certificates of Manumissions

1812

Gloucester County, To wit -

We do hereby certify, that on the First day of August in year of our LORD one thousand eight Hundred and Twelve William Hugg of the Town and County of Gloucester brought before us, two of the overseers of the poor of the said Town of Gloucester and two of the Justices of the Peace of said County his Slave named Jettho Hemrey (a man of couler), who, on view and examination, appears to us to be sound in mind, and not under any bodily incapacity of obtaining a support, and also is not under the age of twenty one years, nor above the age of Forty years.
IN WITNESS whereof, we have hereunto Set our hands, the day and year above written.

Isaac Doughten	)	Overseers of the Poor of the town
Sam 1 Thompson	)	of Gloucester
Amos Cooper	)	Justices of the Peace in and for the
James Matlack	)	said County of Gloucester

[Verso]

Certificate of the Manumission of Jettho   black man late
the Slave of Wm. Hugg.

Certificates of Manumissions

1815.

Know all men by these presents that Whereas Joseph Blackwood Esq late of the County of Gloucester in the State of New Jersey by a certain writing under his hand and seal duly Executed and bearing date the 14th day of July A D 1800 Therin did Grant Bargain and Sell unto his son Samuel Blackwood and to his heirs and Assigns A Certain Negro Girl named Rin or Marinda who was Born a Slave to the said Joseph Blackwood and the said Samuel Blackwood became so seized of said Negro Slave died seized of the same, And Whereas Rebecca Blackwood Widow ~~of-the-said~~ and Administratrix of the said Samuel Blackwood Having taken the said Negro Girl at the appraisement of her Husbands Estate Whereby she became the property of the said Rebecca Blackwood who also died seized of the said Slave and Whereas Joseph O. Clark having obtained letters of Administration of the Estate of said Rebecca Blackwood agreeably to Law and Whereas the said Negro Slave now aged about Twenty one years of age was Appraised to him at Fifty Dollars and the said Joseph O Clark having taken the said negro at the appraisement for the purpose of Manumiting and Setter her Free Now Know ye that I Joseph O Clark having procured from the overseer of the poor of the township of Deptford and two of the Justices of the peace of said County of Gloucester Certificates agreeably to an Act of the Legislature of said State in such cases made and provided Certifying that the said Negro Girl is a proper subject for Manumition agreeably to the provisions of said Act as by the said Certificate will appear Do hereby in pursuant to the Laws of the State of New Jersey in such cases Made And provided amd by these presents Doth Manumit and Set Free from Slavery the said Negro Girl Named Rin or Marinda Aged about twenty one Years in Witness whereof I the above named Joseph O Clark hath to these presents set my hand and Seal the twentieth day of November in the year of our Lord one thousand eight hundred and fifteen 1815

Signed Sealed and Delivered In the presence of   Joseph O Clark   (Seal)
            Thomas Hendry
            Marmaduke Wood

Gloucester ss   Be it Remembered that on the twentieth day of November A D Eighteen hundred and fifteen before me the Subscriber one of the Judges of the Inferior Court of common pleas of said County Joseph O personally Appeared, the within Named Joseph O Clark and Acknowledged that he signed sealed and Delivered the within deed of Manumition, to and for the uses and purposes therein Mentioned. Acknowledged the Day and year above written before

                                            Jacob Glover

(a)

Certificates of Manumissions

1815

20 Nov

[Verso]

            Deed of Manumition for Marina Holland
Recd Novemr 20th 1815 and recorded in the Clerks office of Gloucester
County in Lib W folio 310 of Deeds

                                    Thos. Hendry Clk

Acknowledgement	.50
Recording	.50
	$1.00

Gloucester County to Wit We do hereby Certify that on this twentieth
day of November in the year of our Lord one thousand eight hundred and
fifteen Joseph O Clark of said County Brought before us two of the
overseers of the poor of the township of Debtford and two of the Justices
of the peace of said County his Slave nene Named Rin or Marinda Holland
who on View and Examination appears to be sound in mind and not under
any Bodily incapacity of obtaining a Support and also is not under the
age of twenty one years nor above the Age of Forty years in Witness Whereof we have hereunto set our hands the day and year above written

John Shivers	)	Overseers of the poor
Thomas T Sparks	)	of the township of Dobtford
Thomas Hendry	)	Justice of the peace
Marmaduke Wood	)	in and for the County
		of Gloucester

(b)

Certificates of Manumissions

1816

State of New Jersey

Gloucester County, to wit, We do hereby Certify that on the Sixteenth day of November in the year of our Lord one thousand eight hundred and sixteen, Doctor Samuel Harris of the Township of Newton in said County of Gloucester brought before us, two of the overseers of the poor of said Township and two of the justices of the peace of the said County, a female Slave the property of Isaac Harris Sen. late of the County of Salem, Physician, deceases named Solena, who on view and examination, appears to us to be sound in mind, and not under any bodily incapacity of obtaining a support, and also is not under the age of twenty one years, nor above the age of forty years. In witness whereof we have hereunto set our hands the day and year above written.

Andrew Jenkins	)	Overseers of the Poor of the said
Isaac Webster	)	Township of Newton.
Rich. M. Cooper	)	Justices of the Peace in and for the said
Joel Gibbs	)	County of Gloucester

[Verso]

Manumission Doct. Saml. Harris
Received December 17th 1816 and Recorded in the Clerks Office of Gloucester County in Lib AA folio 431 of deeds.

T Hendry Clk

15/100   Dr. Sam'l Harris

Certificates of Manumissions

1816

Gloucester County to wit We do hereby Certify that on this twenty Day of august Eighteen hundred and Sixteen Eligah Smith of Township of Grate Eggharbour in the said County of Gloucester brought before us two of the overseers of the poor of the Said Township and two the Justice of the peace of Said County his slave Named Christian Cox who on view and Examination appears to us to be Sound in mind and not under any bodily incapacity of Obtaining a Support and also is not under the age of twenty one years, not above the age of Forty years in Witness whereof wee have unto set our hand the day and year above written

Edward Risley   ) Overseer of the poor of the Township
Enoch   his Smith) of Eggharbour
      x
   mark

Thomas Somers   ) Justices of peace in Said County of
John Sharp   ) Gloucester

[Verso]

Christian Cox   Certificate for her Freedom
Jany 7th Paid 75/100

Christian Cox Manumission
Recd. Jany 7th 1817, and Recorded in the Clerks Office Gloucester County in Lib. G. folio 330 of deeds.

Hendry Clk

Certificates of Manumissions

1819

State of New Jersey	Gloucester County, to wit:-

We do hereby certify, That on this twenty seventh day of July in the year of our Lord, one thousand eight hundred and nineteen, William Cooper and Richard M. Cooper acting Executors of the last Will and Testament of Joseph Cooper Esquire late of Cooper's point in the Township of Newton and County of Gloucester aforesaid deceased, brought before us two of the overseers of the poor of the said Township and two of the Justices of the peace of said County. Cornelia McLaughlin Kennedy a female Mulatto Slave, belonging to the Estate of the said Joseph Cooper Esquire deceased, who on view and examination appear to us to be sound in mind and nor under any bodily incapacity of obtaining a support and also is not under the age of twenty one years nor above the age of forty years.
In Witness whereof we have hereunto set our hands, the day and year above written

Cornelius Wiltsee) Overseers of the poor of the
Isaac Webster   ) said Township of Newton

Joseph Rogers) Justices of the peace in and for
Joel Gibbs   ) the said County of Gloucester.

27 Aug. 1819

[Verso]

Certificate of two of the overseers of the poor of the Township of Newton and two of the Justices of the peace of the County of Gloucester for Cornelia McLaughlin Kennedy
Received & Recorded 27 Aug. 1819, Book A page 4 of Manumissions.

Hendry Clk

Certificates of Manumissions - Affidavit

1820

To all to Whom these presents shall come or may Concern I, Simon Wilmer. Rector of the Swedish Lutheran Church at Swedesborough in the County of Gloucester and State of New Jersey Sent Greeting -

Know ye, that I the said Simon Wilmer, for divers good causes and considerations me thereunto moving have, and by these presents do hereby manumit and set free my Negro Slave Lydia Bradly of the age of thirty seven years On Christmas Day next ensueing the date hereof, she being at this time of sound mind, and under no bodily incapacity of obtaining her support. So that neither I myself my heirs executors or administerators can hereafter have claim or demand the said Lydia, or her labour or services as a Slave. In Witness whereof I have hereunto Set my hand and Seal. this Seventeenth day of June. in the year of Our Lord one thousand eight hundred and twenty 1820.

Sealed and Delivered in the presence
of   Thos. Wilkison
        W. Harrison   S. Wilmer (Seal)

State of New Jersey   Gloucester County ss
Be it known that on the seventeenth day of June A Domine Eighteen hundred and twenty before me the subscriber Commissioner for taking the acknowledgement and proof of deeds in and for the said County personally came Simon Wilmer the Grantor to the above instrument of Manumission and acknowledged that he Signed Sealed and delivered the same as his Act and deed to and for the uses and purposes therein contained.
Acknowledged and the Day and year above written before me

                              Tho's Wilkins

[Verso]

30 June 1820
Manumission of Lydia Bradley
Rec'd 30 June 1820 and Recorded in the Clerks Office of Gloucester County in Liba A page 9 of Manumissions

                 Hendry Clk

Certificates of Manumissions

1820

State of New Jersey   Gloucester County   to wit.

We do hereby certfy, that on this Seventeenth day of June One Thousand Eight hundred and twenty. The Reverind Simon Wilmer of Swedesborough in the Township of Woolwich in the County aforesaid brought before us two of the overseers of the poor of the said Township, and two of the Justices of the peace of the said County, his slave named Lydia Bradley who on view and examination appears to us to be sound in mind and not under any bodily incapacity of obtaining a support, and also is not under the age of twenty One years, nor above the age of forty years. In Witness, whereof we have hereunto set our hands the day and year above written.

John Pierson   ) Overseers of the poor of the
Leanard Fisler   ) said Township

Samuel Cooper   ) Justices of the peace in and for
Robt. Littermay   ) the said County of Gloucester

30 June 1820

/Verso/

Certificate Simon Wilmer

Simon Wilmer
Rec'd 30 June 1820 and recorded in the Clerks
Office of Gloucester County in Book A page 8
of Manumissions.

Hendry Clk

Certificates of Manumissions

1824

Gloucester County ss To wit We do hereby certify that on this Eighth day of May in the year of our Lord Eighteen hundred and Twenty six Lewis de Walker and Daniel Leeds Jun'r; Administrators with the Will annexed to the Estate of Richard Westcot deceased of the Township of Hamiliton in said County brought before us two of the overseers of the poor of the said Township and two of the Justices of the peace of the said County two Slaves belonging to said Estate and sett free by the last will and testament of said Richard Wescot deceased named Jim Hall and Beth Seiger who on view and under Examination appears to us to be sound in mind and not under any bodily incapacity of obtaining a support and also are not under the age of twenty one years nor over or above the age of forty years In Witness whereof we have hereunto set our hands the day and year above written.

Job Gybson   ) Overseers of the Poor of said Township of
William Ackley) Hamilton County above said.

James English) Justices of the peace in and for the
Philip Emmel) said County of Gloucester.

[Verso]

Certificate of Manumission of beth Seigers and Jim Hall Recorded on Liber A of Manumissions Folio 22 in the Clerks office of Gloucester County

Smallwood Clk

Paid

Certificates of Manumissions

1824

Know all Men by these Presents, That Whereas Daniel Clark otherwise called Benjamin Clark a black man Slave born in the county of Kent in the State of Delaware in the month of November in the year of our Lord one thousand Seven hundred and Eighty one the Slave of Jenifer Taylor: and by him given & delivered to me the Subscriber sometime about the year of our Lord one thousand eight hundred and ten ab absconded from me, and is now residing in the Township of Newton in the County of Gloucester and State of New Jersey – And Whereas divers benevolent persons have contributed the Sum of one hundred and forty dollars for the purpose of affecting his Manumission – Now therefore know ye That I Ignatius Taylor of the County of Kent in said State of Delaware in consideration of the Said Sum of one hundred and forty dollars to me in hand paid the receipt whereof is hereby acknowledged, and of the further Sum of one hundred and Sixty dollars agreed to be paid by the said Daniel Clark otherwise called Benjamin Clark, and for which I acknowledge the receipt of his bond in Satisfaction of. Do hereby on this sixteenth day of June in the year of our Lord one thousand eight hundred and twenty four Manumit liberate and Set free And by these Presents have manumitted, liberated and set free, the said Daniel Clark otherwise called Benjamin Clark and do hereby fully discharge and acquit the Said Damiel Clark otherwise called Benjamin from all services or demand of Services hereafter to be claimed by me or any person claiming under me –
And I do hereby for myself my heirs executors & administrators ~~and/assigns~~ cavenant and agree to & with the said Daniel Clark otherwise called Benjamin Clark that I have not Sold or conveyed him to any person Whatever and that I have full and perfect authority to Manumit him from Slavery – In Witness Whereof I have hereto set my hand and Seal the day and year above written –

Sealed and Delivered) Ign. Taylor
in presence of)

Interlineations and erasures made before Syning
Jonifer Taylor
J H Sloan

Be it remembered that on the Sixteenth day of June in the year of our Lord one thousand eight hundred and twenty four personaly appeared before me the subscriber one of the Masters of the court of Chancery of the State of New Jersey Ignatius Taylor the grantor named in the foregoing manumission I being Satisfied he is the grantor therein named and having first made known to him the contents thereof who acknowledged that he Syned Sealed and delivered the Same as his voluntary act and deed for the uses and purposes therein named
   J H Sloan M.C.

[Verso]

Manumission of

Benjn Clark
Received July 1 1824 and Recorded in the Clerks Office of Gloucester County at Woodbury in Liber A of Manumissions folio 20 &c

       J J Foster Clk.

Certificates of Manumissions

1824

Gloucester County: /.../ hereby certify that on this first day of July in /........................
.../ Rachel Ireland of the Township of Eggharbour in said County of Gloucester Brought before us Two of the Overseers of the poor of the said Township and two of the Justices of the peace of the said County her slave named Levina Jackson who on View and Examination appears to us to be sound in mind and not under any bodily incapacity of obtaining a support. and also is not under the age of twenty one years nor above the age of forty years IN WITNESS WHEREOF we have hereunto set our hands the day and year above written.

Joseph Scull   )   two of the overseers of the poor for the
Edward Risley   )   Township of Eggharbour.

Jos: Risley   )   two of the Justices of the peace
Daniel Baker   )   for Gloucester County

                                        Recd March 14 1825
                                            j j Foster Clk

/Verso/

Manumission   Rachel Ireland

ACCUSATIONS

1738.

The Accusations of Marmaduke, A Negro Slave Showeth -

Gloucester ss

THAT that ye above Named Negro Slave, Marmaduke on the Sixteenth day of May in the year of our Lord one Thousand Seven hundred & thirty Eight in the Eleventh year of the Reign of King George the Second etc at Waterford in the County of Gloucester in the province of New Jersey did attempt to kill John Collins of Sd. County yoem, and of his Majesty's Leige people, & in ye, Sd. Attempt, with a Certain Instrument called a knife did Grievously wound the Sd. John Collins in the left arm of his body, & in his face, & other harme then & there did, by Reason whereof the life of Sd. John Collins was Dispaired of - - - And also, that ye Sd. negro Slave Marmaduke the time & place above Said did attempt to kill Daniel Garratt one of his Sd. Majesty's Leige people, & in the Sd. Attempt did Grievously wound the Sd. Daniel Garratt in the back with the Sd. knife and other harme to him then & there also did against the peace of the Sd. Lord the King and Contrary to an Act of General Assembly of the ye sd. - - - province in Such cases Lately made & provided &c.

MINUTES OF INQUEST

1748

Glou.) ss
County)   INQUISITION INDENTED and taken at Waterford in the said County Before Joseph Kaighin one of the Corner of our Lord the King for the Said County of the Eighteenth Day of September in the year of our Lord one Thousand Seven hundred and forty eight Upon View of the Body of a certain female Infant ten and there Lying Dead Born of the Body of Nogro Bette being the Sevant of John Borrough of Waterford afore Said upon the Oaths and affirmations of Richard Bidgood Edward Hampton Simon Breach Thomas Hinchman Isaac Matlack Jonathen Oxford Jonathan French Job Siddon James Wheyland George Moor Garrett Burn Joseph Cowgill Nathan Walton John Stocks and Ezechiel Linzey good and Law full men of Said County being Legally Sowrn and Affirmed to Enquire how and in what Manner the said Infant Came to her Death Upon their oaths and affirmations Do Say That (According to the best of their knowledge) the Said Negro Bett Not having the fear of God Before her Eyes but being moved & Seduced by the Instigation of the Devill; on the Seventeenth Day of this instant September At waterford aforesd. in ye County aforesd Did make an Assult upon the Said female Infant then and there being in the peace of God and of our Said Lord the King And that the Said Negro Bett Did feloniously Volentarly ly and of her Malice forethought Strangle and Suffocate the Infant aforesd. with her hands and tieing a leather String about the neck of ye said Infant of which Strangling and Suffocation the said Infant at Waterford afordsd in the Said County Immediately Died and so the Jurors adorsd. Do Say the Said Infant Came to the Death. In Testimony where of the Said Coron'r and Jury hereunto Interchangably Set their hands and Seals the Day and year first above written.

Jos. Kaighm Corner	(Seal)	Job siddons	(Seal)
Richard (his Mark) Bidgood	(Seal)	James Whelan	(Seal)
Edward Hampton	(Seal)	Garrit Byrn	(Seal)
Simon Breach	(Seal)	George Moore	(Seal)
Thomas Hinchman	(Seal)	Jos: Cowgill	(Seal)
Isaac Matlock	(Seal)	Nathan(his mark)	(Seal)
Jonathan Oxford	(Seal)		
Jonathan French	(Seal)	Job Stokes	(Seal)
		Ezekiel Linzey	(Seal)

[Verso]

Inquisition of an
Infant born of Negro Bett

~~John Burr~~
Considerable Smelling

WARRANTS

1738

Gloucester County ss)   To the Sherrife of the County of
                         Gloucester or Deputy.

Whereas this day John Collins Junier brought this Neggor Man before
me John Kay one of the Kings Justices of peace for Glo; County he
saith his name is Marmaduck and that his Master lives in Maryland
& as we understand him his Name is Thomas Masters. The Complaint
ageanst his is that this last night John Collins the Elder found
him in his Seller, Endeavoring to take provission, and to Escape
being taken & Secured have cut & Wounded said John Collins very much
in his arme & Divers other places so that he have lost much bled.
These are therefore in the Kings name To Will and Require you to
Receive, the Said Neygor man and him Keeke in Safe Custody in the
County Goal untill his Master can have knowledge and make Restitution,
or otherwise he be Delivered by due course of Law, for which this
Shall be your warrant, and herein you are Required not to faile,
Given under my hand & sealle this Sixteenth day of May in the Eleventh
year of the Raigne of King George the Second over Great Brittain &c:
Anno Domini 1738

                                                John Kay

[Verso]

Negro Manum.d &c

Warrants

1738.

Gloucester Ss

To the Constable of the Town of Gloucester

G R E E T I N G.

you are hereby Required forthwith to warn John Collings of ye Township of Waterford yeoman and Daniel Garrat of ye Same place Carpenter to be and appear before his Majestys Justices of ye peace for ye County of Gloucester Together with five principal Freeholders at ye Court house at Gloucester on the Eleventh day of July next by ten of ye Clock in ye Forenoon To testify their knowledge Con-cerning a Certain negroes attempting to kill, wounding, and maiming of them ye Sd John Collings and Daniel Garrat, and hereof Fail not, and that you be there Likewise with this precept to Show how you have Executed ye Same, Given under our hands and Seals ye thirtieth day of June Ano Dom 1738.

           John Kay

           Alexr. Morgan

           John Ladd, Junr.

[Verso]

Jno. Collings)
) Warrant.
Daniel Garrat)

NOTICE OF TRIAL

1738

Friend ll   The 24th day of 4th mo. 1738.

Alexander Morgan I Expected the time for trying the Neggor in Custody woud hav been yesterday apointe at Gloucester, but we find the words of the Law is that the Justice that commits him call two of the next Justices, and the three Justices apoint a time for his tryall, & Sumon five freehoulders to meet them at the time & place for his Tryall, So it was found that thou & I & John Ladd was the persons to whome it fee, and accordingly we appointed that we three nominated Should Meet at Thomas Perywebs house the next fourth day at 12 of Clock - to performe that Service, So didires thee not to fail to give thy atendanc for it thou doth apear it will disapoint the whole matter So hoping thou will not fail I conclud & am thy Loveing friend - - -

John Kay

[Verso]

To Alexander Morgan, These -

Notice of Trial

July Ano Domi, 1738.

Province of New Jersey Gloucester County ss

John Kay Alexr Morgan and John Ladd jun'r Justices of our Lord
the King that now is for ye County of Gloucester, being associated
by ordor and appointment of John Kay Esqr at Newton in ye County
af.d./. . ./ye twenty Eight Day of June in ye Twelfth year of ye
reign /. . ./George the Second by ye Grace of God of Great brittain
france and Ireland King defender of the faith etc pursuant to an
act of General assembly of this province Intituled an act forrRegu-
lating of Slaves, To order and appoint a time and place for ye Tryal
of Marmaduke a negroe slave now in ye Goal of ye County afd. and charged
with Divers felonious Crimes - have ordered and appointed that ye
Sd negroe Slave Shall Recieve a Tryal and his offences and Crimes be
heard and determined at Gloucester in ye County afd. on the Eleventh
day of July next and That Ten principal Freeholder of ye County afd. To
Wit Josiah Kay Sam'l Coles Timothy Matlack James Hinchman Isaac Jennings
Sam'l Harrison John Thorn John Hinchman George Ward ye Elder and John
Wood by Summoned to appear at Gloucester on ye sd. Elventh day of July
To ye end that Three of his Majesty Justices of ye County afd. one being
of ye Quorum in Conjuntion with five of ye sd Freeholders may proceed to
Tryall of the abovesd Marmaduke agreeable to Law/. . ./

       John Kay
       Alex.r Morgan

Gloucester ss John Kay/. . ./Randall and Alexander Morgan Esqrs
Justices of Lord/. . ./Gloucester aforesd and also of the quorum
beins/. . ./the Day of July Ano Domi 1738 in ye Twi/. . ./greeable
to ye appointtee at ye above/. . ./above mentioned offender Marmaduke and ha/. . ./inted Jojn Kadd jun.er to prosecute ye sd. Marmaduke and an/. . ./him agreeable to Law.

/Verso/

    The Court being Called and Five Freeholders of
ye sd. County appeared and were Sworn and afirmed agreeable to Law.
To wit
    They being quallofied in presence of ye sd. effender
    prisoner Marmaduke.

MINUTES OF TRIAL

1738

At a meeting of the Justices & five of the principal ffreeholders of the County of Gloucester at ye Court house in ye Town of Gloucester on ye 11th day of July in year of our Lord 1738 in ye Twelfth year of the Reign of King George ye Second etc pursuant to an act of General assembly of the province of New Jersey Entitled and Act for regulating of - - - Slaves.

Present

Saml. Cole)		John Kay)	
Timt. Matlack)	ffree-	Alexander Morgan)	Esqrs., Justices
James Hinchman)	hold-	John Ladd junr. &)	and being of the
And Saml. Harrison)	ers.	Alex.r Randall)	Quorum.
Geo. Ward)			

Marmaduke, a negro Slave he being Accused of Attempting to kill John Collins & Eanl. Garrett of the Sd. County Yeom. the above Named Justices did appoint John Jones Attorney at Law to prosecute the sd. Negro Slave pursuant to an sd. Act of assembly ~~of sd. province Entitled an act for Regulating of Slaves~~.

The Witnesses & persons concerned in the above prosecution not being ready to prosecute ye Sd. Negro Slave, So as to have his Trial on this day, the Sd. Trial is therefore Deferred till to morrow at 10 of the Clock in the forenoon to which time ye meeting of Sd. Justices & ffreeholders is adjourned.

The Justices & ffreeholders met According to Adjournedict
Present as above.

The above named ffreeholders being Qualified According to Law with ye Sd. Justices proceeded to ye Trial of Sd. Negro, & his accusations being Read he pleaded Guilty, & ~~submitted~~ Submits Himself to ye mercy of the Justices & ffreeholders - - -
who having heard ye Allegations & proofs, offered by the prosecutors are of Opinion that ye sd Negro is not Guilty of the attempt above Mentioned in Manner & form as he Stands accured - - - and upon Due Consideration of the whole affairs the Sd. Justices & ffreeholders Do adjudge.
that ye Sd. Negro, Marmaduke Shall be whipt at ye publicks whipping post of Sd. County on ye ~~Twelfth~~ thirteenth Day of this Instant July, & have thirty lashes on ye bare back well Laid on between the hours of 10 and 12 of the Clock in ye forenoon of the Saime Day, and also that ye Sd. Negro have ye like Number of Lases Laid on in Like manner on his bare back one ye Day of the Same Instant and, ~~further~~ also that ye Sd. ~~ffreeholders~~ Negro Slave Do Stant Committed till ye whole Costs & Charges of ye prosecution be paid & Discharged.

Minutes of Trial

1748.

At a COURT JUSTICES AND FREEHOLDERS Met at Gloucester in the County of Gloucester the Twenty Sixth Day of November Anno Domi MDCCXLVLLI pursuant to an Act of General assembly of this province of New Jersey Entitled an act for Regulating of Slaves --------

WHICH said Justices and Freeholders appoints Robert Hathhorne to prosecute etc Who accuseth Negro Betty being the Slave of one John Burrows, That She the said Negro Betty the Seventeeth day of September In the Twenty Second Year of the Reign of our Sovereign Lord George the Second by the Grace of God of Great Brittain France and Ireland King Defender of the Faith etc at the Township of Waterford In the County of Gloucester not having the fear of God before her Eyes but being moved and Seduced by the Instigation of the Devile with Force and arms etc Voluntarily and of her own Malice forethought at Waterford in the County aforesaid in and upon a Certain Bastard Female Child of the Body of the aforesaid Negro Betty born and brought forth then and there in the peace of the said Lord the King being an assault did make &c Same Bastard Child Feloniously and Voluntarily did wound and Evilly Entreat And the Same Bastard Child Feloniously and Voluntarily then and there with a Leathern String fastned and tyed about the Neck of the said Bastard Child then and there Feloniously and Voluntarily with a Leatherer String aforesd so as aforesaid place and Fastened about the Neck of the Said Bastard Child a mortal wound Did give and the same Bastard Child Did Strangle and Suffocate of which Same Mortal wound and Evil Entreatment in the place and position aforesaid the aforesaid Bastard Child at Waterford in the County aforesaid Instantly Dyed and So the aforesaid Negro Betty at Waterford aforesd in the County aforesaid the aforesaid Bastard Child in Manner and Form Aforesd Feloniously and Voluntarily and of her own Malice forethought Did Kill and Murder Contrary to the peace of our Lord the Now King his Crown and Dignity.

    R. HATHHORNE who prosecutor etc. the Defended being arranged pleaded not guilty etc and the procutor in like manner etc and there upon Came the Justice (to Wits.) John Kaighm, Isaac Irames & John Ladd Esq. & the Freeholders likewise came to wits. Robert Stevens Michael Fisher, Peter Rambo, Richard Matlack and Joseph Ellis and the said Freeholders being sworn and Affirmed according to Law by the said Justices to Judge in Conjunction with the Justices of and Concerning the Premises and After hearing the Evidences at will on the part of the proceeutor and the prosecutor, as then Councill for the Defended and Due Deliberation thereupon had the Justice and Freeholders Unammonusly. Do Sign the bill Judge the said Negro Betty not guilty of the accusation whereof she stands Charged And thereupon the Sheriff of the County of Gloucester to Discharge the said Negro Betty out of his Custody.

[Verso]

Evidences
Richd. Bidgood- ---- John Burrows ----- Hannah Borrows
Hannah Bidgood- ---- Phebe Borrow ----- Mary Gill
Defended pleads not Guilty and the Prosecutor in like manner,
Justices and Freeholders having Meet found the Defend Not Guilty

MINUTES OF HEARINGS

1833

Gloucester County ss

Robert Hardcastle) 1833 August 1st on the oath and application of
vs) John Wisener of Philadelphia, Attorney (constituted
Negro Slave, Samuel) in writing) of Robert Hardcastle of Caroline County
and Louisa) in the State of Maryland, who at the same time, produced an affidavit, (agreeably to an Supplement to
an Act entitled "An Act concerning Slaves" Passed the 26th of December 1826)
setting forth that the said Robert Hardcastle, of Caroline County of the
State of Maryland's Negro Slaves Samuel aged about 22 years about five feet
five or six inches high of a dark yellow Complexion, and Louisa is about
18 years of age Common sise of a darker yellow complexion ran away from his
service and labor in the Spring of 1832) Issued Warrants to arrest the said
Samuel & Louisa - John K Cowperthwait Judge &c
1833 August 2nd Isaiah Dill Constable returned the warrants and the Defendants or Negro Slaves Samuel & Louisa in Custody the Attorney of Claimant
examined one witness on oath vis Dr Aaron Hardcastle of Queen Ann County
State of Maryland, says he is the son of Robert Hardcastle the Claimant and
that he was raised and lived with Negro Samuel the person now claimed and
in court from his infancy until about the last two years that the said
Samuel was a Slave to Deponents his father the Son of a Slave woman of Deponents father and ran away from his said Master in Caroline County State
of Maryland in the Spring of 1832 thinks about Easter that the person in
Court now claimed is certainly the Slave of his father and oweth him service
and Labor in said State and is at this time about 23 years of age also that
the said Negro Louisa is Sister to Samuel and Slave to his father by birth
the same as Samuel, ran away at the same time, that she oweth service and
labor to his father the Claimant in the State of Maryland, that she the
person now in custody certainly is the slave that ran away from his father
at the time aforesaid, that she has a scar on the left cheek caused by a
burn that she is maried and is about 19 years of age - Josiah Harrison
Esquire Attorney of Defendants examined one witness, John Wood on affirmation, who saith Samuel came first to live with him about the 6th or 26th
of April 1832, dont know where he came from, never saw or knew him previous
to when he came to live with him, knows nothing of Louisa more than that
she had worked for him last spring a few days - After examining the evidence
and hearing the alligations of the parties I adjudged Samuel & Louisa to be
the slaves of the Claimant Robert Hardcastle and that they both owe him
service and labour and gave a certificate of removal to carry them to the
State of Maryland from whence they fled as follows "State of New Jersey
Gloucester County ss I John K Cowperthwait one of the Judges of the Inferior
Court of Common Pleas of the County of Gloucester do hereby (L.S.) that
John Wisener Attorney (constituted in writing) of Robert Hardcastle of
Carolin County in the State of Maryland having seised and arrested Negro
Slaves Samuel & Louisa, on warrants, and brought them before me hath proved
to my Sattisfaction the said Robert Hardcastle is entitled to the service
and labor of the said Samuel & Louisa under the laws of the State of
Maryland and that the said Robert Hardcastle is therefore authorised to

Minutes of Hearings

1833

remove the said Samuel & Louisa into the State of Maryland from whence they have fled, Given under my hand and seal this Second day of August A. D. eighteen hundred and thirty three J.K.Cowperthwait

I certify the description given above of the Slaves Samuel & Louisa are a correct general discription of them also I believe their ages to be as above stated and that one is a male and the other a female

J K Cowperthwait Judge

I do hereby certify the foregoing to be a fair copy of the record, of the proceedg had before me in the said [. . .] as entered on my Dochet

J K Cowperthwait Judge &c

August 2nd. 1833

[Verso]

Camden N. J.   Paid
   Augt 6   6

         John C. Smallwood Esq
             Clerk of Court
         of Common Pleas, - Woodbury
                              N. J.

         Filed Augs 4 1833
             Smallwood Clk.

Minutes of Hearings

1836

James Miller) 1836 January 27th on the application of Michael Donahower
vs) of Philadelphia Attorney of James Miller Senr. of Sussex
Fillis) County in the State of Delaware, in writing under his hand
and seal duly constituted who at the same time produced
an affidavit of the said James Miller Sen properly authenticated, I issued a warrant to arrest Fillis, a woman rather low and Stout chesnut colour aged about thirty five years who is the Slave of and oweth labour and service to the said James Miller Senr in the State of Delaware from which the said Fillis hath fled and made her escape from her said Masters service and labour sometime in the month of November 1832 the same day Chester Chattin Constable returned the warrant and the aforesaid Fillis (who said her name was Sarah Laws) in court the Claimant by his agent or attorney Michael Donahower was present and neither party demanding any longer time to prepare for trial or requesting an adjournment I examined for the claimant one witness vis John D. Marshal (sworn) of Lewis Town in the State of Delaware, who saith he is the Son in law of the claimant James Miller Senr that he knows the woman arrested now present to be the slave of James Miller Sen for life, that she was born his Slave and oweth service and labour to the said James Miller Sen in the State of Delaware and that she made her escape from the said Millers service and labour in the said State of Delaware sometime in the Month of November 1832, the said Fillis being asked if she had any defence to make offered none, Whereupon I am sattisfied from the proof made that the said Fillis alias Sarah Laws is the slave of the claimant James Miller Sen and under the laws of the State of Delaware from which she fled doth owe labour and service to the said James Miller Sen-

I therefore gave a certificate to the claimants agent to remove said Fillis alias Sarah Laws to the State of Delaware from which she fled, the certificate as follows "State of New Jersey Gloucester County ss. (L.S.) I John K, Cowperthwait one of the Judges of the Inferior Court of Common Pleas in and for said County of Gloucester do hereby certify that James Miller Sen of Sussex County in the State of Delaware by his agent or attorney Michael Donahower of Philadelphia in the State of Pennsylvania properly constitutute in writing having seised and arrested Fillis, and brought her before me hat proved to my sattisfaction that the said James Miller Sen is entitled to the service and labour of the said Fillis alias Sarah Laws under the laws of the State of Delaware and that the said James Miller Senr or his agent Michael Donahower are therefore authorised to remove the said Fillis alias Sarah Laws into the State of Delaware from which she fled the said Fillis alias Sarah Laws is chesnut couloured rather low and stout, aged about thirty five years

Given under my hand and seal at Camden the twenty seventh day of January Anno Domini 1836 J. K. Cowperthwait.

Gloucester County ss

I John K. Cowperthwait one of the Judges of the Inferior Court of Common Pleas in and for said County do hereby certify the foregoing to be a true copy of the record and proceeding had before me in the said case Given under my hand at Camden in said County the twenty eighth day of January Anno Domini 1836

J. K. Cowperthwait

Minutes of Hearings

1836

[Verso]

James Miller Sen
    vs
Fillis
    his slave

Certified copy of the proceedings
had before John K. Cowperthwait
Judge of Common Pleas in the
above case.

Filed February 3d 1836.

    Sailer, Clk

Minutes of Hearings

1836.

Gloucester ss

John T. Taylor Claimant)	1836 December 5th on the application of
vs)	John T. Taylor, of the County of Worcester
Ephraim alias Leven)	in the State of Maryland on his oath Issued
Harmon his slave)	a warrant to arrest his Slave who he alledged
	oweth him service and and Labor in the State
	of Maryland from whence he has fled, whose

name is "Ephraim" (alias Leven Harmon, of the age of twenty nine or thirty years, a bright molatto, with grey eyes, one of his big toes has but a little part of nail on, with a small scar on his back, tolorable well built, not quite so tall Stout or heavy as his Master, is Married) the warrant is as follows "State of New Jersey Gloucester County ss. John K Cowperthwait a Judge of the Common Pleas of said County, the State of New Jersey to the Sheriff or any Constable of Gloucester County Greeting, Whereas it appears by the oath of John T. Taylor that Ephraim (alias Leven Harmon aged about twenty nine or thirty years, a bright Molatto with grey eyes was held to labor or service to the said John T. Taylor of Worcester County in the State of Maryland and that the said Ephraim (Alias Leven Harmon) hath escaped from the labor and service of the said John T. Taylor in the forepart of May last, You are therefore commanded to arrest and seise the body of the said Ephraim (alias Leven Harmon) if he be found in your ~~bailiwick~~ County and bring him forthwith before any Judge of the Inferior Court of Common Pleas of said County so that the truth of the matter may be enquired into and the said Ephraim (alias Leven Harmon be dealt with as the Constitution of the United States and the laws of this State direct
   Witness the said Judge the fifth day of December Anno Domini 1836

        J. K. Cowperthwait (L S)

The same day William Hugg Marshal returned the warrant and the Defendant in Custody, after examining Arthur Nahearn (sworn) and on the confessions of the Defendant, who admitted he was the Slave of the Claimant John T. Taylor, and owed him labour and service in the State of Maryland, whereupon I adjudged him to be the Slave of said John T. Taylor and made out a certificate for his said Master to remove said ~~slave~~ Ephraim to the State of Maryland from which he had fled, the certificate was as follows "State of New Jersey Gloucester County as I John K Cowperthwait one of the Judges of the Inferior Court of Common Pleas in and for said County do hereby certify that John T. Taylor of the County of Worcester in the State of Maryland having seised and arrested Ephraim, and brought him before me hath proved to my sattisfaction that he is entitled to the service and labor of the said Ephraim under the laws of the State of Maryland, and that the said John T. Taylor is therefore authorised to remove the said Ephraim into the State of Maryland from which he fled,
Given under my hand and seal at Camden the fifth day of December Anno Domini 1836
        J. K. Cowperthwait (L.S)

Minutes of Hearings

61.

1836

Gloucester ss

       I the Subscriber one of the Judges of the Inferior Court of Common Pleas in and for said County do hereby certify the above to be a true copy of the proceeding had before me in the said case
Witness my hand December 9th 1836   J. K. Cowperthwait

[Verso]

[Written in pencil]

Proceedings in case of return of a fugitive slave. [Pencil writing ends here]

filed December 10. 1836

                sailer, Clk

Camden N.J.   )
  dec 10   )   Free

   Joseph Sailer Esqr

       Clerk of Common Pleas
          Woodbury
             N.J.

BIBLIOGRAPHY

Acts of the State of New Jersey. "Pamphlet Laws", 1804 - 1837. Bound annually according to years. MacCrellish and Quigley Company, Trenton, New Jersey.

Allinson, Samuel, comp., Acts of the General Assembly of the Province of New Jersey, 1702 - 1776. Isaac Collins, Burlington, New Jersey, 1776. 493 pp.

Cooley, Henry Schofield, A Study of Slavery in New Jersey, in Johns Hopkins University Studies in History and Political Science. Johns Hopkins Press, Baltimore, 1896. 60 pp.

Department of Commerce, Bureau of Census, Negro Population 1790 - 1915. Government Printing Office, Washington, D. C. 1918.

Historical Records Survey, Transcription of the Minute Books, Quarter Sessions and Common Pleas Courts, 1686 - 1739, Gloucester County, New Jersey. Newark, New Jersey. (In preparation - to be published November 1940).

Leaming, Aaron, and Jacob Spicer, The Grants, Concessions, and Original Constitutions of the Province of New Jersey, 1664 - 1702. Reprint. Honeyman and Company, Somerville, New Jersey, 1881. 763 pp.

New Jersey Law Reports, 1845. Issued periodically. State Bureau of Publication, Trenton, New Jersey.

New Jersey Writers' Project, "The Underground Railroad in New Jersey", Bulletin No. 9, 1939 - 40 Series, Stories of New Jersey.

Pennington, William Sandford, comp., Laws of the State of New Jersey, 1703 - 1820. Joseph Justice, Trenton, New Jersey, 1821. 807 pp.

Revised Statutes of New Jersey, 1846. Philips and Boswell, Trenton, New Jersey, 1847. 1155 pp.

Whitehead, William Adee, Fred William Ricord, William Nelson, Austin Scott, et al., New Jersey Archives. 2 series: First Series, 34 vol., 1880 - 1928; Second Series, 5 vol., 1901 - 1917, Newark, Somerville, and Trenton, New Jersey.

INDEX OF NAMES

Names	Pages	Names	Pages
Ackley, William (OP)	29	Clark, Jeffery (O)	14,15
		Joseph O.	38
		Sarahth	18
Baker, Daniel (JP)	30	Clement, John (JP)	23,28,30,
Bates, Daniel (O)	13		31
Dane	<u>13</u>	Cobourn, Ann (O)	19
Bellwood, Edward	<u>1</u>	Coles, Sam'l (F)	53,54
Phebe	<u>1</u>	Collins, John, Jr.	50
Berten	<u>9</u>	John, Senr.	48,50,51,
Bette or Bet	<u>49</u>		54
Betty	2,<u>55</u>	Combs, Solomon (O)	22
Biddy	6, <u>7</u>	Cooper, Amos (JP)	32,33,37
Bidgood, Hannah	55	Joseph (O)	42
Richard	49,55	Richard M.(JP)	38,42
Blackwood, Jno (JP)	17	Samuel (JP)	44
Jos. (JP)	12	William	42
Joseph (O)	38	Cowgill, Joseph	49
Rebecca (O)	38	Cowperthwait, John K.	
Samuel (O)	38	(Judge)	56,57,58,
Borrough, John (O)	49		59,60,61
Borrow, Phebe	55	Cox, Christian	41
Borrows, Hannah	55	Creighton, Hugh (O)	13
Bradley, Lydia	<u>43</u>,<u>44</u>	Crim, Peter (OP)	12
Breach, Simon (F)	49		
Bricke, Saml (OP)	24,25,26		
Brown, Job (OP)	33	Deval, Abratham	18
Jonathan (OP)	12	Sarah	18
Burn, Garrett	49	de Walker, Lewis	45
Byrn, Garrit	49	Dill, Isaiah (Con)	56
Burrough, Benjamin (JP)	36	Donahower, Michael (AL)	58
Burrows, John	55	Duffield, Merinda	<u>34,35</u>
Caldwell, James B. (O)	22,34,35	Early, John (OP)	14,15
Carpenter, Thos. (JP)	14,15	Eldradge, Wm. (O)	20
Chambers, Ben	19	Ellis, Joseph (F)	55
Champion, Joseph (JP)	23,28	Emmel, Philip (JP)	45
Chattin, Chester (Con)	58	English, James (JP)	45
Clark, (Clk)	24,25,26	Ephraim	<u>60</u>
Daniel		Evens, Joseph (OP)	23,27,28
alias Benjamin	46		
E. (Clk)	9,10,11,		
	13,14,15,	Fillis	<u>58,59</u>
	16,17,21,	Fisher, Michael (F)	55
	22,23	Nences or Nenus	<u>36</u>
Jeffery (JP)	10,11,12,	Pero	<u>27,28</u>
	16,20,31	Fisler, Leonard (OP)	44

63.

Names	Pages	Names	Pages
Fittermary, Rich'd	29	Hooper, Levi (OP)	21
Flora	<u>13</u>	Hopkins, Jas, (JP)	21,31
Folwell, Samuel (O)	18	James (Judge)	27
Foster, J. J. (Clk)	6,7,47	Hugg, George W. (A)	26
Frank	<u>5</u>	Joseph (O - JP)	9,13,16,
Freeman, Rachel	<u>18</u>		17,27,35
Tenvi	<u>21</u>	William (O - Ma)	37,60
French, Jonathan	49		
		Ingersull, John (O)	8
Garratt, Daniel	48,51,54	Irames, Isaac (JP)	55
Gibbs, Joel (JP)	40,42	Ireland, Rachel (O)	47
Gill, Mary	55	Ishmael	<u>29</u>
Githens, Thomas (OP)	13		
Glover, Jacob (Judge)	38	Jackson, Levina	<u>47</u>
John (OP)	9	James, English (JP)	45
Gooden, Jacob (OP)	14	Jenkins, Andrew (OP)	40
Goodin, Jacob (OP)	15	Jennings, Isaac (F)	53
Green, Joseph	27	Joe	<u>19</u>
Sarah	20	John	<u>2</u>
Griffyth, Jno (JP)	16	Johnson, Dianna	<u>3</u>
Groff, Garret (OP)	10,11	Emaline S.B.	<u>4</u>
Gybson, Job (OP)	45	Phebe	<u>4</u>
		Sill	<u>3</u>
		Jones, John (AL)	54
Hall, Jim	<u>45</u>	Justice, Nicholas (JP)	29
Hampton, Edward	49		
Hardcastle, Aaron (Dr.)	56		
Robert (O)	56	Kadd, jun.er, Jojn	53
Harker, Jonathan (JP)	22,24,25,	Kaighm, John (JP)	55
	26	Joseph (Cor)	49
Harmon, Leven	<u>60</u>	Kay, John (JP)	50,51,52,
Harris, Isaac, Senr.			53,54
(O - Physician)	40	Josiah (F)	53
Samuel (Dr.)	40	Kenard, Saml (JP)	13,16
William	19,52	Kennedy, Cornelia	
Harrison, Josiah (Atty)	56	McLaughlin	<u>42</u>
Sam'l (F)	53,54	Robert (O)	1
Samuel W. (O)	24,25	Kille, Samuel (O)	5
William	34,35,43		
Hathhorne, Robert	55		
Hemrey, Jettho	<u>37</u>	Ladd, jun'r. John (JP)	51,52,53,
Hendry (Clk)	3,4,5,		54,55
	12,40,41,	Lawrence, John	22
	42,43,44	Laws, Sarah	<u>58</u>
Thomas (JP)	38,39	Leeds, Jun'r. Daniel	45
Heritage, John (OP)	9,16,24,	Linzey, Ezekiel	49
	25,26	Lippincott, Jacob (OP)	10,11
Hinchman, James (F)	53,54	John (OP)	35
Thomas	49	Nathan (OP)	17
Holland, Marinda	<u>39</u>	Samuel (OP)	29
Homan, Vanderver (OP)	<u>35</u>	Littermay, Robert (JP)	44

Names	Pages	Names	Pages
Louisa,	<u>56</u>,<u>57</u>	Rin	<u>38</u>
		also Holland, Miranda	<u>39</u>
		Risley, Edward (OP)	41,47
Marmaduke	<u>48</u>,<u>50</u>,<u>53</u>,	Rodger	<u>12</u>
	<u>54</u>	Rogers, Joseph (JP)	42
Mary Ann	<u>6</u>	Rose	<u>22</u>
Marshal, John D.	58	Rowand, John (OP)	23
Masters, Thomas	50	Robert (OP)	31
Matlack, James	1,3,4,		
	24,25,26,		
	32,33,37	Sailer, Joseph (Clk)	59,61
Hannah (O)	12	Samuel	<u>56</u>,<u>57</u>
Richard (F)	55	Scull, Joseph (OP)	47
Timothy (F)	53,54	Seiger, Beth	<u>45</u>
Matlock, Isaac	49	Selena	<u>40</u>
Mickel, Isaac (O)	23	Sharp, Edw'd (O)	2
Middleton, Joseph (OP)	36	John (JP)	41
Miller, James, Senr. (O)	58,59	Sharper	<u>23</u>
Mina	<u>30</u>,<u>31</u>	Shivers, John (OP)	39
Miranda	38,39	Shores, Jeffery	<u>14</u>,<u>15</u>
Mitchfield, George		Jane	<u>10</u>,<u>11</u>
Huggins	<u>32</u>,<u>33</u>	Siddons, Job	49
Moore, George	49	Sloan, Joseph (JP)	36
Morgan, Alexr. (JP)	51,52,53,	J. H. (M.C.)	46
	54	Smalwood (Clk)	8,45,57
		Smith, Ceasar	<u>24</u>
		Eligah (O)	41
Nahearn, Arthur	60	Enoch (OP)	41
Nancy	<u>5</u>	Smithers, Thomas	<u>25</u>
		Smothers, Fanny	<u>27</u>,<u>28</u>
		Smoers, Thomas (JP)	41
Ogden, C. (Clk)	1,2,28,	Sparks, John (O-JP)	9,14,15,
	29,31,32,		17,18,21
	33,35,36	Thomas T. (OP)	39
Charles (JP)	33	Stevens, Robert (F)	55
Oxford, Jonathan	49	Stratton, James (O)	29,34,35
		Still, Cupid	<u>26</u>
		Tabbey	<u>16</u>
Paul	<u>6</u>	Stocks, John	49
Paul, Samuel (OP)	29	Stokes, Abigail (O)	30,31,36
Peryweb, Thomas	52	Jacob (O)	27,28,30,
Phebe	<u>1</u>		31
Pierson, John (OP)	46	Job	49
Pine, I. (JP)	20	John (O)	27,28,30,
			31,36
		Susaneth	<u>17</u>
Rambo, Peter (F)	55		
Randall	53,54		
Redman, Thomas (OP)	13,27	Tabbey	<u>16</u>
Reeves, Biddle (OP)	22	Tayler, Wm. (O)	<u>11</u>
Thomas (OP)	20,21		

Names	Pages
Taylor, Ignatius	46
John T. (O)	60
Jenifer (O)	46
Susannah (O)	10,11
Thompson, Peter (OP)	16
Samuel (OP)	37
Thorn, John (F)	53
Toby	<u>7</u>
Tod, William (O)	6,7

Vilet	<u>8</u>

Walton, Nathan	49
Ward, George (F)	53,54
Webster, Isaac (OP)	28,30,31, 36,40,42
Westcot, Richard (O)	45
Westcott, Samuel B.	8
Whelan, James	49
Wheyland, James	49
Wilkins, John (JP)	9,10,11
Hannah (O)	12
Tho's	43
Wilkison, Thos.	43
William, Joseph	19
Wilmer, Simon (Rev)	43,44
Wiltsee, Cornelius (OP)	42
Wisener, John (AL)	56
Wood, James C. (OP)	20
Jeremiah (JP)	22
John (F)	53
Marmaduke	38,39
Mary (O)	32,33